1 MONTH OF
FREE
READING

at

www.ForgottenBooks.com

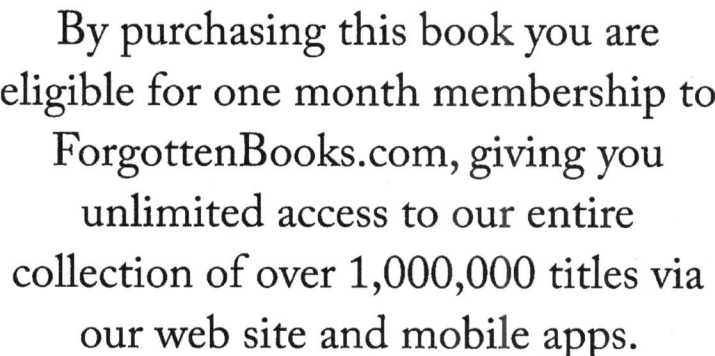

By purchasing this book you are eligible for one month membership to ForgottenBooks.com, giving you unlimited access to our entire collection of over 1,000,000 titles via our web site and mobile apps.

To claim your free month visit:

www.forgottenbooks.com/free582224

ISBN 978-0-428-97100-7
PIBN 10582224

ACTA VICTORIA

January 1914

BOOK ROOM PRINT

Mention "Acta." Advertisers appreciate it.

Victoria College

In Federation with the University of Toronto

OFFERS TO STUDENTS

1. A compact college life in a commodious and beautiful modern building, provided with all the latest conveniences for healthful work.

2. A large staff of College Professors, composed of men with thorough European training and ripe experience as teachers.

3. Admission to all the lectures and laboratories of the University. The staff of the University, together with the professors and lecturers of the federated colleges, constitutes the largest faculty of Arts in the Dominion and one of the most efficient on the continent.

All University examinations, prizes, scholarships, honors and degrees, are open to our students on equal terms with those of any other college. There are further prizes, scholarships and medals offered in our own college.

Two commodious residences for women students afford every modern advantage for health, comfort and refined social life. A course of physical training is given under an accomplished directress, and a women's gymnasium forms part of the equipment.

Excellent facilities are afforded both in the University and college for post-graduates reading for the degrees of M.A. and Ph.D. The Faculty of Theology gives complete instruction in the course leading to the B.D. degree.

Applications for rooms in Burwash Hall will be received at the College Offices.

R. P. BOWLES, M.A., D.D., LL.D., President

Mention "Acta." Advertisers appreciate it.

ACTA VICTORIANA

Contents for January Number

Published monthly during the College year by the Union Literary
Society of Victoria University, Toronto.

Winter

Acta Victoriana

| VOL. XXXVIII. | TORONTO, JANUARY, 1914. | NO. 4 |

The Sea Bird

On the slopes of the wind I careen and slant,
    Out and over the sea:
The cloud is black, the gray waves pant,
    And surging is the sea.

The wind is a shrieking host this hour,
    And the storm is her company.
Ripped, yellow, and haggard these heavens lower
    While I move under free.

I scream in the swirl of the driven mist
    Over the face of the sea;
I hover and swoop and rise again—
    And the heart of the storm calls me!

Down, down, down,
    Dizzying, dark, long rush.
Heart of the storm! Heart of the storm!
    Heavens that press and crush—
      —Back to my rocks I flee!

Mutter and moan and sob of the sea,
    Thunder and bellow and roar,
White fanged ones that leap to catch at me
    Weltering upon the shore—
      —Back to my rocks I flee!

A. L. PHELPS, B.A.

The Civic Playground

The question of what to do with the children of any modern city to keep them from vice, improve their environment and provide them with adequate playing space, is one that is just now receiving much attention in every city in Canada and the United States. A new spirit is abroad in these lands, which has changed the municipal mind and opened the civic coffers. To-day it is not difficult to interest the officials of any city or to obtain access to the taxpayers' tribute in the name of the playground for city children. A generation since we had not discovered the need of such a work; a decade later we saw the need but made no definite effort to meet the situation; to-day we realize that the children of our cities must be provided for and the Civic Playground Department is the result of that realization.

When our cities were small and their population was nearly all Anglo-Saxon, when the vacant lot was noticed on almost any street, there were few children to care for; there were many places where they could play, and the type of child we met was one that could play, instinctively, the Anglo-Saxon games. But the sudden development of the city, the influx of foreign children, the congestion in foreign quarters, the placing of the apartment, the store or the factory where the boys and girls had so long had their ball-fields, race-courses and gathering places, all meant a new order of things in the life of the boys and girls. There were traffic regulations to be observed and street by-laws which forbade any games on the roadway. Policemen were constantly correcting and forbidding, and citizens raved at those who walked on their close-cut lawns. What were the boys to do? They sought the alley, the sheds, barns or vacant houses, and in these places tried to find their natural birthright —a place to play.

Play is instinctive, natural, wholesome and essential to the normal child. It reacts in three ways on the character of the boy or girl. It gives a stronger, more normal physique, it trains the eye, mind and spirit to alertness and speed, and it helps the child to gain a proper perspective.

But the play of no two peoples is alike, and when the children of twenty races gather in an area one mile square, as is the case in almost any city in Canada to-day, we find that the majority of the foreign children do not know how to play. If they do they cannot play with the Anglo-Saxon, for there seems to be a caste line between the foreign child and the native-born, even as the native parents scorn the " dago " and " sheeney." It is the business of the common play-area to break down this division and to weld the whole into one type-figure—the Canadian boy or girl.

" What," you ask, " is the method of procedure with which the authorities begin ?"

Let us take a typical case as an example. When a city ward shows unmistakable signs of congestion and crowding and there is a marked need for special accommodation for the boys and girls of that district, a piece of ground is purchased, cleared and fenced, and is treated with sand to produce a good playing surface. The area is then measured off into small squares and apparatus for each square is designed—a set of large swings for this corner, a giant " stride " for that portion there, a huge sand bin for this part, a ball diamond in the middle, a system of teeter-boards, a pavilion for the little folks, baby hammocks for the tiny ones, a May-pole for the dancing of the larger children, basketball courts, bowling areas for tenpins, a large toboggan slide of polished wood—these and a score of other devices are installed and made ready for the wide-eyed onlookers.

Then the question of the supervisor comes to the front. He must be a man of peculiar temperament, able to command the instant obedience of any child, yet able to play with any as one of themselves. He must have a patience that can pass through a hot July day when the area is crowded with shrieking, heat-tortured little folk. He must have a vision of the possibilities of the playground work so that he realizes what patient direction, example and decent environment can do with tenement and foreign children. He will be judge, ruler, playmate and adviser of the children who attend his ground, or else he will be nothing but the man with the keys and will be a complete failure.

The question of a director for the girls must also be considered, and a young woman of like temperament is searched for. Her duties are almost as numerous and diverse as those of the chief supervisor, but she has the comforting knowledge that he is held responsible and shields her from the heaviest part of the season's work, namely, the organizing, preparatory and executive burdens. And now the plant is ready to begin operations, to throw open its gates, to admit the little army of boys and girls, the future men and women, who are to be cast into the great mixing pot of strenuous play. Through the medium of their play hours, by means of organized, carefully directed play, simple rules of manly and womanly conduct in a true child-kingdom of democracy, the newcomers of our population, the little children of the slum district and the more carefully cared for middle class boys and girls will reach a common understanding of the real ideals of the Canadian child. A new world will open up before the European children and we will begin to form that long looked for type of being, the child of all nations, —the Canadian boy and girl.

For weeks past crowds of children have been gazing through the fence with wide, staring eyes, excitedly arguing with each other about the various pieces of play apparatus, the prices of admission, the qualifications for admission, and a score of other views of the question. In one district the report grew that only Protestant children could come in. When they followed the supervisor down the street and asked him if that were true, and he replied that any children who were willing to be obedient had full rights to the use of all apparatus, the Catholic children could hardly credit their ears. Then the Jewish children feared they would be shut out, only to find that everybody was to be made equal in every respect.

The day finally dawns when the ground is to be formally opened. A band is to play, some speeches are to be made, and the City Council will formally turn over the ground to the playground directorate. For days the excitement of the children has been growing. On this day they flock to the play area from all corners of the Ward. Such yelling, such laughing, such squeals of delight as the teeters see-saw up and down and the swings soar up high among the trees, or while the long arms of the giant " stride " throw the little bodies in a great flat ellipse about the big steel pole. Two ball games, played with the big, soft " indoor " ball, are in progress, another group

of children are racing in a basket ball relay race, while in a
secluded corner under the big maple trees fifty little tots are
solemnly building castles or moulding layer cakes and wonderful turnover pies from the dampened black sand. What a scene
it is. How those "kiddies" are enjoying themselves. To many
it is almost too good to be true. No more for them the filthy
alley or the dangerous roadway. They have a place to play,
and, wonderful to relate, all kinds of "great" and "grand"
things to play with. Do you wonder they come to spend every
possible moment on the grounds? Would you have enjoyed
such a privilege in your youth? To the writer such a thing
would have been a never-ending picnic.

So this goes on every day. Ball leagues, team races, sew-
ing classes, musical afternoons, story hours and even a Court
of Justice are organized. The rules for the operation of the
ground are posted, and also the scale of punishments for infrac-
tions of these regulations. In all cases of misconduct the
regular court procedure is followed, Judge, plaintiff and defend-
ant make their formal statements, and the former decides upon
a verdict. The punishment is nearly always expulsion for a
fixed number of days or hours, and while usually the cause of
copious tears and protestations, it generally results in the future
observing of the regulation in question. Bullying, swearing,
cheating, lying, disobedience or damage to apparatus are the
chief offences provided for in the playground statutes, and by
the time a month has slipped by there is a very marked decrease
in their number.

In such a small space the large attendance is rather difficult
to handle, and, to facilitate supervision of each part of the
apparatus, officers are chosen from the ranks of boys and girls.
These are each given charge of one piece of apparatus, and are
held responsible for the proper utilization of that piece. Thus,
if there is overcrowding, lack of watchful care or selfish "hang-
ing on" after the regulation time limit has expired, the officer
in charge regulates the difficulty and sees things more smoothly
again. These officers are chosen for their leadership and common sense qualities, and are either a great success or a flat
failure in their positions. If a supervisor has good officers he
is pretty sure of a smooth season, but if they prove a failure
his troubles are certainly multiplied.

The question naturally arises as to how much land such a work requires. Is it possible to buy enough land in a congested district to do useful work without enormous expense? In answer to such 'queries we would instance one play area in a Canadian city where the attendance this summer in 78 days was 15,206. That area measures exactly 84 by 120 feet. Of course there was overcrowding, certainly the directorate was hampered for lack of space, but good results were achieved despite the lack of room. Surely a piece of land that size is available in any congested district, and, equally surely, there are men who will give it to such a cause.

But if there is one feature of a civic playground that strikes the onlooker above all others, it is the remarkable democracy that prevails, and in few words let me set forth this feature in concluding this article. We all realize the peculiar conditions which obtain in our cities, how twenty to thirty nationalities are found among our little folks. We also realize there is a certain caste and race prejudice which is present amongst them. In a land like ours, with our problems, needs and opportunity, we must break down such barriers and establish a great common democracy. In the older minds and lives this is a very difficult thing to do, but with the children no real difficulty is experienced. True it is that in playground work there is, at first, a clan and clique of the races each unto itself, but in the excitement and fervour of strenuous play this is all forgotten. The day soon comes when Ikey, the Jew, is chosen first on the team because he can play first base better than Johnson, the Canadian candidate. Soon we see the most cosmopolitan gathering on ball diamond, soccer field or basketball court that one could well imagine, and the boys and girls who were accustomed to fear taunts, jeers and slurs hurled at them because of their race and tongue, are delighted to be received on terms of absolute equality. So the Slav, the Jew, the Italian or the Armenian is given a new sense of his own worth, and soon he loses the furtive manner with other boys, and life in Canada becomes to him really happy and worth while.

Such is the work now being done in the civic playgrounds of Canada, and surely the work calls for the sympathy of the real Canadian. Surely such efforts are worthy of the encouragement and support of the thinking public. Certainly the day is not far distant when from one coast to the other all the children of our great cities will be given the privileges and advantages of supervised and carefully-directed play areas, controlled by the municipalities.

J. H. FENTON, '15.

Pro Patria*

" Now, who these tales of many forms would read
　Must have his soul awaked to sympathy."

With these lines an old friend and student of mine begins his conclusion, in which he turns to his reader from a group of allegories in which he has tried to body forth the fair day he sees in prospect for his land—old Erin, once loved of saints and poet, but so long the prey of the foreign conqueror, that when another bard among her sons greets her as " the willow of the many-sorrowed world," none need stop to ask his meaning.　At last a fairer day seems to be dawning for her, at last the dream of Ireland, ruled by the Irish and for the Irish, seems likely to be realized.　And one of her sons, one sprung from the very heart of the Green Isle, sets before us in this little volume his hope for the future of his Motherland, using the stanza of Edmund Spenser, the poet who, over three hundred years ago, pleaded with his fellow English in Ireland to make the best of the land of their adoption.　In four poems— " Erinensis," " Reciprocus," "Zenia" and " Euvenesis "—Mr. Pearson presents us with pictures from different points of view of Erin's sorrows and the purification won from them. In the first he describes the English conquest, that plunges her into misery and " seeks to wreak on her eternal war."　But

" The thought can never die; the ages pass;
　Fell destiny is destined in its course
　To suffer fell defeat; the cruel mass
　Must conquer often, yet so much of force
　Lies in the smallest gem of thought, resource
　To rise again eternal is; afar
　The sun shines down to aid it: from remorse
　It springs to greater things—the raging war
Has purified the soul a better life to share."

It is James Stephens who in his "Crock of Gold" assures us that man need not fear Destiny, but that Destiny shrinks in

*Poems by J. J. Pearson, Wm. Briggs, Toronto, 1913.

fear before man's will when stirred to oppose it. In "Reciprocus" we have a picture of the battle for liberty, and the standard abandoned at the crisis, a betrayal that has occurred again and again in the struggle for Ireland's freedom. A long expiation follows for the standard bearer who shrank from the final effort, an expiation ending only with his death. In "Zenia" the West comes to aid the East, and the poet breaks off with the words, "'Peace, peace,' the angel said, 'hath come for evermore.'" He has withheld the conclusion of the poem, for the struggle is not yet over, but his concluding words augur his confidence in its speedy close. In "Euvenesis" we have a purification of Venus, which seems intended to give us a picture of the reform of morals in the Green Isle, of which she is so justly proud. To these four pictures is subjoined an antilogue in which is traced the rise of the powers that have at various times swayed the world, ending with the gentle rule of Him who sought to bring peace and rest for men. That Mr. Pearson has not studied Spenser for nought will be clear to all who read his poems; his verse has somewhat of the full calm sweep of the Elizabethan master, passing on with slight regard for tyrant and monster, but with eyes firm set on the final victory of the good and true. Something we feel, too, of the interest of the master in the story which is the medium of his teaching, a story whose interest is such that it tends to obscure the truth it is intended to teach. We find, too, in Mr. Pearson's work, the same interest in "aged accents and untimely words" that was so strong in his master. Some of his words are new to me, and one, Euvenesis, seems a hybrid, but one so fair that I am loath to censure it. In the shorter poems with which he begins his little volume, he shows his interest in the poets who have used Spenser's stanza, in Byron, Burns, Keats, and Shelley. Those who remember the garden where rest the body of Keats and the heart of Shelley, will sympathize with our poet in his thought of the God "whose love doth mark the sparrow's fall," and may recall Gilder's lines:

"Something there is in Death not all unkind;
   He hath a gentler aspect looking back:
   For flowers may grow in the dread thunder's track.
And even the cloud that struck, with light was lined."

I would not leave the volume without mention of the verses beginning, " Awake once more! the sunlight falling tender," in which he has voiced anew the Horatian rule for a brave life,

Omnem crede diem tibi diluxisse supremum.

A. J. B.

Leaves in Late Autumn

Blown leaves, strown leaves,
   In the whirlwind's path,
Tracing mystic circles,
   Summer's aftermath.

Light leaves, bright leaves,
   Frolicking and gay,
Dancing their death dance,
   Hurrying away.

Torn leaves, shorn leaves,
   Tattered by the gust,
Settling on the greensward,
   Forming earth's dust.

Lost leaves, tossed leaves,
   Quiet and at rest,
Covered in a snow shroud
   'Gainst Earth's bosom pressed.

H. Holgate, M.A., Dec. 18, '13.

A Great Council of the Kingdom

M. P. Smith, B.A.

Even though great conventions and conferences of the kind have been conducted before, the one in session at Kansas City, Mo., from December 31st, 1913, to January 4th, 1914, in some respects may be called the greatest. The forces of Christendom face a larger proportion of the non-Christian world than ever before. The character and existing beliefs of these lands have acquired a new definiteness and exactness. The political situation demands the prayerful sympathy of the Christian nations with an appeal of urgency. The social changes in these partially occupied fields afford an unprecedented opportunity and challenge to aggressive service.

The responsive co-operation of Kansas City residents made it possible to entertain 5,031 accredited delegates from 755 institutions of learning, which was the largest assembly of the Student Volunteer Movement in history. Without the support of the students, professors and friends of Victoria College, our full quota of delegates could not have been sent. Provision was made that twenty might go from our own halls.

The special train arranged for the Canadian Delegation left the Union Station at 7.45 a.m., December 30th, and proceeded over the G.T.R., via Sarnia, to Chicago. Needless to say, the daily routine of the vacation period was somewhat disturbed in many homes that morning by an early breakfast. Punctuality proved absolute in her control, as no one was left behind. They were a jolly crowd on board, who sped their way across Western Ontario. Friendships were renewed, and new acquaintances were made between members of the different faculties and colleges.

After dinner was served, very few seemed to be interested in the Michigan landscape, through which they were passing. The missionaries, board secretaries and church officials were unconsciously claiming the attention. They were at the centre of small groups of eager listeners in every car. The receptive spirit of the company soon sought the power and blessing of One, Who is greater than man. The rattle of the train became

more audible, as the stillness became more intense. All were
silently pleading for the spirit, guidance and direction they so
much needed.

The Santa Fe Railway officials carried out their determina-
tion not to take second place to a Canadian railway in provid-
ing comfort and ease of travel. The transfer from train to
train was easily effected. True to student life, some love to
disturb, while others seek rest. But before Engine 519 had
threaded its way through the many lights and semaphores and
over the network of switches, the quietness of the coaches which
followed reminded one that it was night time. However, long
before daylight, the blissful slumbers of berth occupants, as
well as residents of a small Missouri city, were broken by a
foreign college yell given by lusty early risers. Almost before
the faces were washed and the hair brushed, it was announced
that the train had stopped at the Union Station in Kansas
City.

One of the features long to be remembered was the perfec-
tion of every detail in organization. It is hard to imagine how
any one could even take a wrong turn. Guides were stationed
along the way with cards bearing full directions. The usual
crowds at the registration desks were entirely dispensed with.
The Boy Scouts of the city acted as personal directors in securing street cars and transfers to lead the delegate directly to
the address upon the card of introduction. Imagine a train-
load of Canadians being comfortably located in different homes
within two hours of the time of arrival without any one suffer-
ing apparent tax or strain.

Before the appointed hour of the first session the east hall
was well filled. The Canadian delegation occupied seats of
honour directly before the speaker's table in the front of the
main floor. The gavel in Chairman Mott's hand brought
silence and order to the thousands before him. The great conference was now open.

Speaker after speaker probed the individual heart and life
to locate self-seeking and false motive. The feeling of con-
demnation rippled as a great wave over the audience. The
" treasures of earth " were far outweighed by " the riches of
love in Christ Jesus." There were new heights of service to

be scaled, that stood out prominently before many. All past endeavour became insignificant in view of the possibilities of the future. New standards and ideals were set up and new resolves made before the first meeting was dismissed. In passing out, one wondered what had caused such a change. The meeting was quiet. There was nothing to excite—no emotional appeal whatever. Speer had driven home his message with great invisible power.

Wonderful as was that first session, each succeeding one seemed to convey an added wealth. The plan of each was distinct and unique. Each one had a new message and contribution. The interest grew and increased. So great was the demand for seats that at some sessions hundreds of delegates were not admitted, because they reached the hall a few minutes after the general public were admitted. The spirit of the interior penetrated the very walls, and lodged in the hearts of the clamoring multitudes without. It was interesting to notice the psychological effect the crowd had upon the tall men with the batons. At first they stood in the dignity of their positions to drive the expectantly angry mob away, but when the words of "Stand Up, Stand Up for Jesus" and "Faith of Our Fathers" echoed around the outside walls, their batons dropped to their sides, and they saw the working of Power not enforced by civil law. And it may not be false to say that not a few of them were troubled in spirit.

The Association Quartette was enjoyed and appreciated by all. Their message of song was specially fitting to each occasion. If by chance the message of an address was not grasped, the selection that followed it always made it clear. The continuity of the messages was most pronounced.

Although many distinguished men were always present on the platform, the latitude of speakers was not wide. The four who figured most prominently were Mott, Speer, Eddy and Zwemer. These men poured out treasure after treasure to the large audiences.

It was Saturday night (January 3rd) that so many thousands were unable to secure entrance to the hall. It might be called "Statesman's Night." Canada was represented by Dr. J. A. Macdonald, who was referred to as the "Gladstone of

Canada," His masterly method and persuasive force in dis-
cussing " The Strategy of the Nations " will be a living memory
for years in the minds of students from north, south, east and
west. William Jennings Bryan then held the crowd spellbound
for an hour with his matchless, rippling oratory. His words
displayed great national foresight in the leavening of the
nations with Christian truth.

The announcing of the budget and the raising of the funds
came as a surprise to everyone. Mr. Mott told of his recent
world tour, describing many incidents that happened when he
and Mr. Eddy were in India and Japan, and when they were
joined by Mr. Brockman in China. Every sentence was effective and telling. At the close of his address, the ushers passed
cards to each delegate. These were collected two minutes later,
bearing the amount of the subscription. Those were moments
when many wished they were millionaires. There was no
appeal for money. The facts were stated, and the delegates
felt themselves a part of Mott's work, because they had prayed
for him when he was in the East, and felt that in contributing
they were doing something to carry out the watchword, " The
Evangelization of the World in this Generation." In a very
few minutes $113,000 was contributed. Many realized a new
blessing through genuine sacrifice.

Opportunities were provided by which one might have
personal interviews with return missionaries from different
fields. Board secretaries were besieged on all sides by enquirers, who wished to know how and when they might be per-
mitted to go to the various fields of service. Much of the spare
time was spent in examining the exhibit of literature. It was
most complete and extensive, and in charge of trained workers,
who never grew weary of explaining and making clear obscure
points. One of our own delegates remarked, while in the
exhibit hall, " Everyone here is handing out real dope." A
mere glance at the galleried seats, with their many groups of
enquirers and listeners, revealed the statement as true.

The conference bristled with opportunities for measuring
the extent of the Student Movement. To see the large body
present so deeply interested in the extension of the Kingdom
and to realize that they were but a small representation of the

great army who were not present, did much to set forth its might and magnitude. But it became world wide, after hearing the fraternal delegates from the similar movements in the British Isles and China. The appeals that were made on behalf of the students of neglected and less fortunate lands brought home to each delegate the sense of a wider and greater brotherhood. The walls of a narrow provincialism were fairly shaken from their foundations and many a world citizen was born, with a new conception of personal power and influence, that might be wielded in a wider sphere.

Perhaps the most interesting service was the closing one held Sunday evening (January 4th). Dr. Ross Stevenson, the vice-chairman, came to the front of the platform and read the honor roll, while all sat in memorial silence with bowed heads. Of the fifty-three who had paid the price with their lives in the past four years, five were from Toronto. When the name of a classmate or dear friend echoed throughout the stillness of the hall, it caused the muscles of the face to stiffen, the hair to move as with an electric presence, and the heart to burn and glow with Christian admiration. Mr. Mott then requested those who propose to sail within the next year to stand. In answer to this call something like one hundred young men and women rose to their feet. During those moments it is safe to say that not a few thought of the words,—

"Like a mighty army, moves the Church of God,
Brothers, we are treading where the saints have trod."

The impressions of that occasion will surely be immortal.

Before the final prayer of benediction all were reminded of the importance of the "Morning Watch," in keeping the larger vision of service and sacrifice foremost in the mind and heart. The closing words were burning their way into many lives long after the convention had broken up into delegations and had dissolved into personal units. Each one was convinced that theirs was the opportunity of living a larger life than before, and of multiplying the forces of the Kingdom by incarnating the spirit of genuine service into the student body.

"Student Control" in Early Cobourg Days

It was Dr. DeWitt, the unfailing friend of ACTA Editors, who hinted that there were some historic things in the Library vault which should be of interest to ACTA readers. So we hied over to ask Prof. Lang what strange and ancient curiosities he might have hidden behind that ponderous door. His face brightened at the question, and we surely were shown.

Before our wide-open eyes was displayed the charter of Victoria College, well preserved in spite of its age, and on it we spied the name of Sir Francis Bond-Head. Here was a Calendar of Upper Canada Academy for 1840—the earliest Calendar of the college known to be in existence. From the inner precincts of the vault was brought an ancient Account Book of a pioneer Methodist organization, and it bore the date of 1796—only 117 odd years ago. These and more we saw, and of them something may be written for later ACTAS. But what interested us most was a curious little booklet on whose cover page someone had written "By-Laws of the Upper Canada Academy, Cobourg, 1839." On the back cover of the book was written, now scarcely decipherable, a ponderous Greek word— just to show posterity, doubtless, that our predecessors were oppressed even as are we.

Curiously, yet almost timidly, we turned the pages to see what rules and regulations stern confined the erring feet of the students of the Academy within the paths of rectitude and duty away back in 1839. Perhaps we might glean helpful suggestions for the House Committees of Burwash Hall. Possibly there might be discovered the source of inspiration of the rules at Annesley. At least we might expect invaluable hints for the aid of our redoubtable Students' Council.

We had thought to quote a few of the by-laws, but so interesting are they all, so clearly reflecting the methods and customs of their day, that we venture to print herewith, for the edification of all who read, a fairly complete reproduction of the rules which governed our predecessors in those early days.

By-Laws.

I.—The hour of rising is, in the summer, 5; in the winter, 6 a.m.; of retiring, 9.30 p.m. Prayers shall be regularly attended in the Lecture Room with becoming reverence, in the morning by the resident students an hour after rising, and in the evening, at the close of the daily recitations, by all the students.

II.—About nine hours are devoted each day to study and recitation, viz.: the time intervening between morning prayers and breakfast, 9 and 12 a.m., 1 and 4 and 7 and 9 p.m. During these hours each student is required to remain in his room, except such as the Faculty may find necessary to have under their immediate supervision. Music and all species of interruption are prohibited in study hours.

III.—No student will be allowed to go to the village, or take excursions in the neighbourhood, except between breakfast and 9 a.m., unless in extraordinary cases, when permission must be obtained from one of the Faculty. Permission will be rarely granted to spend the evening out, and that only when it is well known where and how the students will occupy it—in which case they must always return before the 9 o'clock bell rings and report themselves to one of the Faculty.

IV.—None of the young ladies or gentlemen entrusted by their parents or friends to the care of this institution are at liberty to contract debts, or to dispose of anything in their possession, without the concurrence of those upon whom its immediate superintendence and direction devolve. Students are expressly prohibited from frequenting any tavern or grocery where intoxicating liquors are sold, lounging about any store or public place, or remaining in them longer than their business requires.

V.—Each student will be held responsible for the appearance and furniture of his room, which he is to sweep out and put in order every morning before prayers, and in which he shall at no time permit or indulge in any boisterous or disorderly proceedings. The rooms shall be at all times accessible to the teacher, who shall visit them as often as may be necessary.

VI.— * * * Students are strictly prohibited from intruding upon the lands or property of the inhabitants, or meddling with their fruit, etc., without permission.

VII.—All indecencies or improprieties, such as writing on the walls or any part of the premises, loud talking or playing in the halls or rooms, smoking, throwing water or dirt from the windows, entering the doors with dirty shoes, slovenliness of person, rushing to or from meals, unbecoming conduct at table, and the odious practice of spitting on the floor, are strictly prohibited.

VIII.—Bringing firearms or powder, throwing stones or other missiles on the premises, playing ball in the yard, etc., are all absolutely forbidden.

X.—The ground to the west of the edifice is appropriated as a place of exercise for the young ladies; the rear and playground for the young gentlemen. More effectually to preclude all intercommunication between the young ladies and gentlemen, their conversing, corresponding, or in any way associating together, save in the case of brothers and sisters, and that by a written permission from the Principal and Preceptress, is especially interdicted.

XIII.—In addition to ordinary letters, the students are *required* to write to their parents or guardians at the close of each term. These letters shall be examined by one of the teachers, who will insert a report of their scholarship and moral deportment.   *   *   *

XIV.—All resident students are required to attend public worship on the Lord's Day, both in the forenoon and afternoon, under the ministry their parents or guardians may prefer. Neither riding nor visiting for pleasure on the Sabbath, going abroad in the fields, frequenting the village, collecting in each other's rooms, engaging in any of the ordinary week day diversions, making any disturbance, nor lounging about the premises; in a word, no species of conduct by which that hallowed day would be desecrated, will be allowed.

XV.—As the foundation of that order so essential in an institution for the intellectual and moral training of youth, due respect to the officers is imperative upon all under their tuition and care. Any student who shall contumaciously resist any of the officers shall be punished as the circumstance may require.

XXII.—As a precautionary measure against fire, it is deemed necessary to require that during the time stoves are allowed in the rooms, the room doors be left unlocked in the night that the stoves may be inspected by a person appointed for that purpose. Any student detected in kindling fire after the stoves have been inspected, unless demanded by sudden indisposition, will be punished as the circumstances may require.

Surely, with a code of regulations so minute and extended as these, " the wayfaring ' student,' though ' fresh,' need not err therein." Would it be in order to suggest that, purely for experimental purposes, the residents of Burwash Hall be subject to the by-laws of the old Upper Canada Academy for a space, say, of twenty-four hours?

Concerning the Conversazione

On Friday evening, December 5th, the college was *en fête,* the occasion being the Annual Conversazione. All day the building was the scene of chaos and activity in preparation for the big function. But by evening order was restored and the halls presented an appearance at once beautiful and inviting.

The reception took place on the second floor, followed by a concert rendered by some of the best vocal and instrumental talent in the city. Particularly pleasing was Arditi's song " Il Bacio," by Master George Branton. D'Alexandro's Orchestra, in two divisions, that on the first floor being concealed by an artistic arrangement of palms and flowers, supplied music for the promenades.

With the prospect of hearing such an excellent programme as was provided, and with other arrangements so attractive, why did the "Conversat." not receive better support from the student body? The lack of interest on the part of the students this year seems to be without precedent. The old friends of the college responded to the invitation of the committee with all the spirit of former years. But, while the attendance of students and their guests has usually been about 430, this year there were only 250. Must we conclude from this that the greatest of Victoria's social events no longer appeals to the students as a whole; or did the accidents of circumstance so conspire as to prevent such a large number from attending this particular function? Was the lack of interest due to the various other receptions held during the fall term? Can it be that the fear of overcrowding, or the dislike of the greater formality usually observed at such gatherings, kept the students away? The answer to these questions must of necessity be somewhat vague and unsatisfactory since no general expression of opinion has been heard on any one point. However, provision was made which would have eliminated overcrowding to a very great extent at least, and the event was no more formal than it has been for many preceding years; and less formal than some fifteen or twenty years ago. The lack of interest appears to have been general, not confined to any particular year or class. But whatever may be the reason for this apathy on the part of the student body, a definite expression of opinion should be obtained from it before again undertaking the heavy liabilities involved in carrying to a satisfactory completion such a function as the Conversazione.

—'14.

Le Misanthrope

There is a cave not distant, where the snows
Of surly winter, driv'n by every blast
Through the bare, stiffening underbrush, and past
The overhanging mosses careless close,
Fell far within, and into masses froze
That heed no stir of spring; but, firm and fast,
Shielded by nature's clust'ring growth, they last
To spite the summer sunshine, and the rose.
Within the heart lie winter's frozen snows,
While all abroad the birds of summer sing.
Life's teeming joys but weave a sombre gate
To close the chilly portal; and the rose,
Flower of happy love, in vain may fling
Her fragrance there—until it is too late.

W. F. B., '14.

"In Memoriam Roberti".

H. J. GOODYEAR, B.A.

The unique and worthy institution, the Bob, will, we hope, perpetuate the memory of its founder.

The Bob Committee of 1911, however, decided that some tangible and lasting memorial to the memory of Robert should be erected somewhere in the college buildings.

After much deliberation and a year of waiting the beautiful dial in the library has been installed. The Bob Committees of 1911-12-13 have contributed to the fund in about equal proportions.

The Presidents' of the respective committees were Messrs. W. M. Smith, ('14) ; P. W. Wallace, ('15), and W. Zimmerman, ('16). The committee of design, purchase and installation were Messrs. H. J. Goodyear, ('13) ; W. M. Smith, ('14), and W. J. Little, ('13).

Messrs. Sproatt and Rolph are deserving of appreciation for a subscription of ten dollars, and for a discount of seventy-five per cent., owing to simultaneous and extensive orders from the firm that made the dial, the discount on all the orders having been applied on the cost of the clock.

We are very grateful also to Dr. Bell for his apt and excellent Latin rendering of the homely English which we handed him.

Of Robert himself it is fitting to say a few words.

Robert served the college as janitor for twenty years. Though his duty was humble, his soul was noble and his thoughts were high. He was, in the truest sense, a gentleman. The professors admired him and were his friends. The students of the higher years and he were " pals." To the Freshmen he was a father and listened patiently and tenderly to their tales of woe. He had no enemies; and those who knew him best liked him most.

We who knew him will always cherish his memory. But the clock in the Library will lead many to ask: " Who was Robert?" We hope there will always be someone to answer: " He was a man honored by all and disliked by none."

The Athletic "V"

The meeting of the Athletic Union, held not long ago, to consider the matter of granting the Athletic " V " to the holder of the tennis championship of the college, and the vote of the society refusing to amend the constitution, so as to render this possible, has opened the discussion among some of the students as to whether the clauses regulating the conferring, as it were, of these " New Year Honors " is not in need of some revision.

In granting the " V " the Union has endeavored to place before the students an incentive to development along athletic lines. Of course, some basis upon which it was to be given had to be fixed, and those responsible for its institution naturally turned to Inter-Faculty Contests and decided that it should be granted to all those who, either as individuals or members of a team, had won an event or championship for the Collegian Inter-Faculty Competition. Such are the conditions under which the honor has been and still is, given.

Now it is quite obvious that if it is granted at random and becomes too common around the College that the object will be defeated for which it was instituted. This its originators clearly foresaw; and they wisely tried to guard against any such result by making the Constitution definite on this point. Their successors also, on the Executive, from year to year have zealously watched it; so that we may safely say that it is, at present, a reward of some distinction and that every student in the college is desirous in a varied degree of attaining it. Thus far the " V " has been a success. The tendency, however, has been for some to regard the Athletic Society Constitution as a more or less sacred document and, as a result, in their efforts to keep the law to the letter have forgotten the spirit.

We must never fail to remember that the bestowal of this honor is only a means to an end. Development and exercise should be the goal at which every participant in athletics is striving. The winning of a championship is not always the " summum bonum " of man. In rewarding, then, those who have excelled in any branch of sports it is quite clear that no hard and fast rule can be drawn. But it is natural that it should be based on Inter-Faculty Competition. For besides displaying that a player has excelled, honor is brought from outside to the college. This course, as a general rule, has been wisely followed; but the mistake has been made in failing to recognize, first, that all athletics are not on the same basis and secondly that the winning of a championship in an Inter-Faculty Series cannot be in every case an absolute and final test.

That the basis of competition in all branches of athletics is not the same is quite evident. Take Rugby, for instance. Where there are fourteen members on a team and rarely more than twenty-five members in the college taking an active interest in this sport, there are only two teams at most in the college and the second team, as far as contests are concerned, is practically a dead letter. Thus the first team is driven outside the college to get any competition whatsoever and, naturally, going into the Inter-Faculty Series, the winning of the championship in these contests is the reasonable place to reward them. With a game like tennis, however, it is quite different. This is by far the most popular sport in the college and thus we do not need to go outside for competition; so that we have our regular tournament each fall. Now the only way it is possible, in tennis, to win the " V " is by winning either the " Singles " or the " Doubles " in the Varsity open tournament. In the singles, however, a reward is already offered; for the winner of this event is always granted his " T "; and, as every student regards the winning of the " T " as a much higher honor than that of the " V " it is quite obvious that the extra incentive produced by the " V " is reduced to nothing. Thus, then, the only competition in which the " Vᵢ " exerts a stimulus is in the doubles. But as the players do not take much interest in this, being far more anxious about the singles, the doubles are hardly ever won and thus it is exceedingly rare in comparison with other sports that a " V " is granted for tennis.

Furthermore, a tennis player may obtain his "V" by winning the doubles in the Varsity Open Tournament, while the winner of the Victoria " singles " or the champion of the college, who is, perhaps, a far superior player, is refused it. That there is some unfairness here and room for readjustment of the conditions of winning the " V," is quite apparent. The common argument against this extension of the " V " is that to give it for anything but Inter-Faculty Competition is to make it common and cheap. But how can it become common by giving it to the champion player of the college when it only means that one player out of fifty or more who are playing annually receives it? And how can it become cheap when we consider that the standard of playing at Victoria is practically on a par with University College and certainly superior to any of the others. We had two out of five representatives on the team that went to McGill. We won the Varsity open singles last year and the doubles this year. This is surely sufficient to prove the quality of our playing and that the champion in tennis is probably as proficient in his game as any Rugby or other man that ever gets his " V." Yet in spite of the fact that there are more playing and more keen interest taken in tennis than any other game around the college, this sport has fewer representatives winning their " V " than any other form of athletics around the college.

It is high time, then, that the college tennis champion at least should receive this honor; and whether or not it should be extended to the winner of the tournament is another point that should be discussed and settled at the next annual meeting of the Union. The writer would himself advocate this also.

That Inter-Faculty Competition alone ought not to be the final and absolute test may also be quite readily seen. We ought to have some latitude in which to reward the man who gives time and energy throughout the whole of his college course toward the encouragement and development of some sport in the college and who, it may be, though himself a player of high standing, has not been fortunate enough to have been on a championship team. There are also " Vic " players who have been members of the University team where there is individual competition, such as swimming and diving or track athletics. Only last year a man who had won success in diving and who represented the whole University at O. A. C. was refused his " V " because it was not Inter-Faculty Competition. Such an attitude of the " authorities " only tends to make players entirely indifferent about striving for it.

What new basis do we propose? We would suggest that the Constitution be amended, first, so that the college tennis champion be assured of his " V " and that the matter be taken up at the next annual meeting of the Union as to whether or not this honor shall be extended to the annual winner of the

" singles " in the tournament. Second, that the champion in the Annual Field Sports be given the " V." Here is a field where it can do good missionary service. Track athletics are at present at a low ebb in the college. They need some encouragement to revive interest, and there can be no doubt but that the donation of the " V " will provide some decided additional inducement. Moreover, it will mean only one more " V " being annually obtained.

Third: we would suggest that a clause be inserted in the constitution to enable the Executive to reward with a "V" the man who has performed meritorious and distinguished services for College athletics, though he may not have happened to have been on a team that has won a championship, yet possibly in numerous finals. For instance, any player who becomes expert at handball and succeeds in arousing enthusiasm in it throughout the whole student body and in elevating it to a much higher plane in sporting circles, should be able to be honored if the students think fit. We should have this privilege and power, even though it is never used. There is no reason why the constitution should forever tie us down.

These suggestions, if adopted, will put the "V" on exactly the same footing as the University "T." Let those who say that, if they are put into effect, it will become common and cheap remember this fact and recognize that there is no reason why this objection should be more true of Victoria than of Toronto University. Yet has the "T." become worthless, and not worth striving after? On the contrary is it not a great distinction? Are there not some around the University who would rather win it than a scholarship? Furthermore, it may be objected that such powers in the hands of the executive are bound to be abused at the hands of popular "demagogues" who cannot get it any other way. We would again take such students to the Varsity Athletic Executive and ask them if such has been the case in that body which possess these powers? It is true that there is no one around the College like Dr. Barton to exert a restraining influence. But if it is felt that some such person is needed, why not call in the aid of the Honorary President of the Society, or some chosen professor around the College, if it is thought fit, who will have the power of veto or advice in such a case. The whole experience in the past has been for the students zealously to guard the " V." Those who, if the suggestions given here were put in practice, would have the greatest opportunity for abuse, have been in the past most faithful and anxious to preserve its force. But they have erred, probably through the fault of the constitution, in being inclined to too much rigidity.

In conclusion, the dissatisfaction that has been expressed around the College concerning the donation of the "V" clearly shows that some of the students do not yet regard it as being on a perfect basis. It is surely time that this matter be taken up and threshed out. The suggestions given above express in a "nut-shell" how it can be improved. There can be no doubt that the University has a better system than we, and we cannot do better than follow them in every detail.

R. R. FLEMING.

ACTA VICTORIANA

EDITORIAL STAFF, 1913-14

W. M. SMITH, '14 - - - - - - - Editor-in-Chief,

MISS I. H. McCAULEY, '14 } Literary.   MISS E. A. DAVIS, '15 } Athletics.
H. G. ROBERTSON, '14   R. R. FLEMING, '15

H. A. FROST, B.A., Missionary and Religious.   J. SPENCE REID. '14· Scientific.

L. G. HUTTON. '15 Personals and Exchanges.   MISS H. F. HAY, '15 } Locals.
                                              H. BENNETT, '15

BOARD OF MANAGEMENT:

J. A. R. MASON, '14· Business Manager.

H. C MYERS, '15, Circulation Manager.   G. R. WEBER, '16· Assistant Business Mgr.

ADVISORY BOARD:

PELHAM EDGAR, Ph D   C. C. JAMES, C.M.G., LL.D.

TERMS: $1.25 A YEAR; 20 CENTS THE COPY

Contributions and Exchanges should be sent to W. M. SMITH, Editor-in-Chief.
"Acta Victoriana"; business communications to J. A. R. MASON, Business Manager,
"Acta Victoriana." Victoria University, Toronto.

EDITORIAL

We have entered upon the year 1914. For some of us who have been accustomed to associate the year with our names it has more than usual significance as the year of our graduation. For these it is the year so much looked forward to, yet often half-feared, seeming sometimes so long delayed, and again too quickly come. For all of us it is a year of renewed opportunity where success, mediocrity or failure are as ever before us as paths which lie pretty much within our own power to choose.

Some time ago at Convocation Hall the minister said that the greatest necessity of the average man is a trained will. This, we believe, is especially true in the case of the college man, for he to a degree greater than most classes of people, can do as he chooses. The bank clerk has his stated hours when he must be at his work; the mechanic must be " on his job " or lose it; the business man finds it imperative that each day find him at his office, even the farmer must resolutely face his daily round of duties.

But with the man at college it is different. His lectures are being given. He may take them or not at his pleasure. There are afternoons and evenings for study if he pleases. There are books in the library which await but do not compel his reading. He may do exactly as he chooses. Examinations seem

remote; duties and pleasures of many sorts intervene and his
own will is the absolute king of his life.

Have all of us sufficient will-power to study continuously
and consistently for two consecutive hours? How many of us,
having mapped out a day's work, are able to follow it out accord-
ing to schedule? How few of us can read history, for instance,
page after page, without "wool gathering"! How many of
us can do any school work successfully and efficiently except
under pressure?

It is a fact that most college students must bring all their
will power to bear in order that their studies shall receive the
necessary attention. But we maintain that it is in this very
effort of will in face of no compulsion other than our own
best interests, hazily realized, that one of the great values of
college training is to be had. The college student whose will
is so trained that he can apply himself resolutely to study for
a fixed and proportionate time each day, rigidly excluding all
extraneous thought during the period, is not only doing justice
to his college course, but is also acquiring character and a fixed
habit of life which will enable him to "make good" anywhere.

The College Man's Attitude Toward Politics

Is it too much to expect of the undergraduate that he shall
have at least a fair working knowledge of the public issues of
the day? One of our professors of English in Toronto University recently said that he knew but little about present-day
English poetry, because his time was so taken up in studying
and teaching English poetry of the past. It would seem simi-
larly that many undergraduates under the pressure of studies
which involve a knowledge of past history and issues can find
little time to keep posted upon present-day issues and happen-
ings. In the Literary Society this term an effort is being made
to stimulate greater interest in public questions by having them
made the text of motions introduced as Government business.
It is hoped that by thus adding the spur of party rivalry the
issues will be debated with greater intelligence and increased
spirit. The experiment merits at least a thorough and con-
scientious trial, and will be watched with much interest by all
concerned.

Rightly or wrongly, let us take it for granted that every undergraduate should have a fair knowledge of the political issues and movements of the day. Then what should be his attitude of mind toward them? We hear much to-day about the necessity for independence in politics being fostered at our universities. To what extent should that independence be carried? It would appear that the party system is the most practicable and efficient method of carrying on government which has as yet been devised. If it be an evil, it seems nevertheless to be a necessary evil, and there is every indication that Canadian governments will be carried on under the party system for many years to come. This being the case, why should college undergraduates be urged unceasingly to preserve an attitude of independence? Independence carried to the extreme is like democracy carried to the extreme: either would make the carrying on of government well-nigh impossible.

We have every right to demand that in the party caucus there shall be given the freest scope to individual and independent opinion upon each and every issue which may arise for discussion. But once the party in caucus has decided upon a common compromise policy it is both imperative and legitimate that, in the great majority of cases, the independent viewpoint shall be subjugate to this policy. But there are times when issues arise which involve great principles. There are occasions when the interests of the nation demand that the life of a government shall cease or that its general policy be reversed. Then it is that the individual is justified in not bending to the dictates of party but in asserting his independence, and in the fact that at such times such independence does assert itself lies the salvation of the party system.

We believe that the college man should face the political situation as it is. There is no very good reason why he should not be a party man. In fact he needs training in merging his individual opinions with those of the majority of his party. The one thing essential, the one thing which he must make sure of, is that party sentiment shall never dictate when inviolable principles are called in question.

It is to be hoped that in the not far distant future our political parties will come direct to the universities for men to help lead and direct their forces. And it is only right that our undergraduates prepare themselves as well as they may to be true party men in the best possible acceptance of the term.

From the "Grad" in College

VICTORIA COLLEGE, JAN. 7TH, 1913

Dear Mr. Editor:

Since you insist that I tackle a " Grad's " letter, I see nothing for it but to " tackle " a few of the varied types of college
men I see about me in the University. Doubtless my classifi-
cations will clash with those of everyone else, but we'll hope
that in such clashes some interest may be found to lie.

One of the most pretentious yet uninteresting groups which
it pleases me to differentiate is that of the student-recluses. I
wonder do they live to study or study to live? Apparently
both. They seem never to lose hope that they will be able
actually to read all the books prescribed for their courses; they
even continue despairingly to assail the hundreds more which
the professors recommend. You may see them emerging from
the caverns of the stackroom, sitting sleeplessly at library tables,
burning the midnight incandescence, but you will look in vain
for them on the campus, at the Lit. or in committee room—so
vast is their passion for knowledge.. First-class honors is their
pillar of cloud by day, scholarships their pillar of fire by night.
Their personality is lost in " studiosity." Sometimes I wonder
if their instructors are really enthusiastic over these indefatig-
able delvers. Being optimistic about college professors, I am
glad to say that I have my doubts.

A very harmless, almost ludicrous, group comprises that
select fraternity of true-blood sports, whose chief claim to
notice rests in their being not half so " sporty " as they believe
themselves to be. . Tremendous Titans in dissipation are they
—as they resolutely believe. Into what depths of deviltry do
they not go! Why, they actually smoke, attend all the dances
and most of the " shows," pour afternoon tea, do terrible execu-
tion among fair maids' hearts and sometimes carry canes. In
very truth they are the elite, living in a select, scented atmosphere apart and distinct from that breathed by the common run
of students. For the ordinary college organizations and interests they cherish an elaborate disdain. But all unbeknownst
to them, they are as unimportant in the college life as they
deem it unimportant; they are virtually ignored by the great

mass of students of whose existence they maintain such careful innocence. In due time they will graduate, having spent twice as much of their dad's money as they needed to do during their course and, for aught I know, having been the admiration and despair of nine-tenths of the "co-eds" en route. With the devout hope that this percentage is over-great, I leave them.

It is with a sense of welcome contrast that I turn to the group of real genuine sports, whose one fault is that they love the campus " not wisely but too well." With all their exhilaration and energy they turn from fall sports to winter sports, play them all well and squarely, but, somehow or other, they don't quite give their lectures a square deal. But they are dandy fellows, with plenty of brains as well as brawn, and while it may require the chastening effects of even a year lost to bring about a more balanced division of work and play for some of them, there is every hope for the truly good sport.

Then there is a group of men for whom I feel genuinely sorry, clever, capable, all-round fellows who are fighting a losing game under the weight of burdens of their own devising. When they entered college they had in view only the activities of their academic work, and for the first year or two they have headed their respective lists. But, shall I say, unfortunately, they possess the qualities of leadership, the personality that comes to the front, and they have become ambitious for the honors which their classmates have been only too ready to accord. And so each succeeding year has witnessed, in their case, a heightened pressure of outside work, a heavier strain to hold their academic standing until after a final year overburdened with college work not pertaining to their academic course, they face a mediocre graduation.

Are they to be the more praised or pitied? Certainly they cannot hope both to have their cake and to eat it. They have won and lost. If of philosophic turn they will find compensation for the loss of academic honors which might have been theirs, in the college honors conferred by their fellows and in the value of a wide and varied college experience. They stand no chance side by side with the student-recluses, for no matter how extensive and successful their efforts for their college may be in the various student organizations, in debate contests or on the athletic field, the Faculty, even as Shylock of old, must say: "We cannot find these things; they are not so named in the examination papers."

Perhaps once in a decade there comes a student with intellect so keen, with ability so outstanding and with method of work so systematic and orderly that he wins out in every sphere of college life. Keep your eye on him, for he is destined to lead a nation.

In Victoria we have a very interesting group of men whom I might characterize as the XXX brand theologues. They are splendid men, of deep, thorough-going convictions who can never quite understand the point of view of an Arts man, and he in turn will never even try to understand theirs. The college should strive to understand these men, not to change them. They generally have seen too much of real life to enter very strenuously into our play-life down here. They never lose track of the fact that their college training is not an end in itself but simply a means whereby they can better equip themselves for the life outside. Many Arts men do forget this entirely. But, remember, I wouldn't speak thus favorably of all our theologues. I have my own opinions of some of them.

Well, I guess the great majority of us are still left unclassified. We are plain, ordinary college men with brains enough to worry along, money enough to scrape along and laziness enough to slide along. We study enough to get indifferent standing, play some game well enough for exercise, catch a place on an occasional committee, cheer at debates, eat well and feel generally pleased with ourselves. Our personality is not so unattractive as to make us unpopular while our common sense holds us in our place. We are the sturdy yeomanry of the college and as such let us be content.

Has anyone been interested enough to notice that I have not attempted any classification of the "co-eds"? Let these form a worthy subject for a worthier "grad." I venture to believe that they would scarcely admit of classification but—I really know nothing about them. And there is much of regret in that final statement, too.

But all this last is to no purpose, so I close.

Very truly yours,

TRESDEKA.

Personals and Exchanges

Exchanges

"The Lyrics of Robert Bridges" is the title of an article by Professor Taylor in the *Queen's University Journal Supplement*. Although brief, and by no means exhaustive, the account is charmingly suggestive of the work of England's latest Poet Laureate, a man, we suppose, practically unknown to Canadians until his appointment to that honor in June last.

The writer attempts no biography or characterization of his subject. He treats him simply with respect to his lyrical work, illuminating his somewhat meandering remarks with copious extracts from the poet's writings. To suggest the atmosphere under which he works he paints for us the home of Mr. Bridges, the wide countryside, the southward aspect, the view of Oxford's spires and towers, the glimpse of river and corn-field, pine-woods and garden, these in the distance, and near the house long wavy grass, "ancient farm-yards," oaks. "And," he writes, "it is out of these things around this house that Mr. Bridges makes his poems."

"Mr. Bridges," writes Professor Taylor, "is a true poet of nature, he saddens and rejoices with all weather." And then come several quotations: trees and butterflies. flowers, snow, farm scenes, winter jollity, the commonplaces of poets; one feels that we have not here a writer of the highest rank, and yet a reading of these few extracts convinces one that he is a true poet, of real simplicity and a sincere sympathy with the things of nature; not passionate, yet quietly responsive, and honestly so.

But Mr. Bridges has another side, a deep human sympathy as well as a nature-sympathy. One cannot refrain from quoting from his verses "On a Dead Child":

"Perfect little body, without fault or stain in thee,
With promise of strength and manhood full and fair!
    Though cold and stark and bare,
The bloom and charm of life doth awhile remain on thee.
To me, as I move thee now in the last duty,
Dost thou with a turn or gesture anon respond,
    Startling my fancy fond

With a chance attitude of the head, a freak of beauty.
So quiet! doth the change content thee?—Death, whither hath
    he taken thee?
To a world, do I think, that rights the disaster of this?
    The vision of which I miss.
Who weep for the body. and wish but to warm thee and awaken
    thee?
Ah! little at best can all our hopes avail us
To lift this sorrow, or cheer us, when in the dark,
    Unwilling, alone we embark,
And the things we have seen and have known and have heard
    of, fail us?"

As Professor Taylor observes: " By his very quietness of
contemplation—he is calm enough to note how, by chance, the
head lies in an attitude of life—he makes one feel how unsearch-
able is death. Yet, having looked into its measurelessness he
is not afraid."

But there is joy, too, and activity—" sounds of hasty run-
ning feet and glad voices mingling in the cool, dark, morning
air "—in some of his lyrics—

    " Awake, my heart to be loved, awake, awake!
    The darkness silvers away, the morn doth break
    It leaps in the sky: unrisen lustres slake
    The o'ertaken morn. Awake, O heart, awake!"

" Men Were Deceivers Ever "

Yes, it had come to that. They must part and that at once.
From casual acquaintanceship they had gone rapidly through
the stages of increasing friendship, and now . . . . .
The thought of it was enough to make the gods shed tears,
but sternly they both approached the last scene of all. He was
a motorist! No more was known. She was a sweet girl undergraduate on holiday. They had met, as one sometimes does in
the wilds. It was evening, dark was approaching. He had
run out of matches and his lamp would not light. She had
given him her box of vestas, but still the lamp would not go.
They had discussed the matter amicably together, and she had

discovered that he was bound for the hotel she was staying at. That was the beginning. . . . This was the end.

"Farewell, Angelina," he said. "I may see thee no more."

"Ah, say not so, Alexis," she breathed, "be not so cruel."

"It must be so. Duty calls. I must get me gone forthwith. Tempt me not. Read this note." Draws a dainty colored envelope from his pocket. "My fiancée arrives by the afternoon train." Dashes for the door.

She, smiling softly, soliloquizes, "Well, perhaps it is well that he should go before John comes. They might not have got on well together, and he might wonder where I developed Angelina." Smiles again.—*The Student.*

So cold was the night,
   And her cheeks were cold, too,
Though it wasn't quite right.
So cold was the night,
And so sad was her plight,
   That I—well, wouldn't you?
So cold was the night,
   And her cheeks were cold, too.

        Amherst Literary Monthly.

We are glad to welcome the first numbers of the *Literary Supplement* to the *Queen's University Journal* and *The Gleam,* the new publication of the United College (Manitoba College and Wesley College) Winnipeg, and to wish their promoters all success in their undertakings. The following exchanges have also been received: *Oxford Magazine, McMaster University Monthly, The Student, The Gateway, Notre Dame Scholastic. O. A. C. Review, Albertus, University of Ottawa Review. Argosy, Macdonald College Magazine, Stanstead College Magazine, Allisonia, St. Hilda's Chronicle,* and *St. Andrew's College Review.*

Personals

Another of Victoria's graduates has won honors on the continent. Rodger J. Manning, of '06, has been awarded the degree of D.Sc. (Doctor of Science), by Bristol University. The achievement is remarkable in that the honor was attained in a shorter time than ever before. Dr. Manning is now studying at Griefswald, Germany, under Dr. Otto Dumroth.

The many friends of Mr. F. G. Buchanan, '13, classical master in the Calgary Collegiate Institute, will be glad to learn that he has recently been appointed Inspector of Schools, with headquarters at Hanna, Alta.

On Tuesday, December 23rd, Miss Ella A. McLean, of '02, daughter of Dr. S. C. McLean, was united in marriage to Rev. P. G. Sutton, at the home of the bride, Spencerville, Ont. The couple will make their home, after February 2nd, at Smoky Lake, Alta., where the Rev. Mr. Sutton has charge of an Austrian Mission.

Mr. R. M. Edmanson, '12, of Calgary, Alta., paid a flying visit to the College just before the Christmas vacation.

A wedding of interest, especially to graduates of '11 and '12, to many of whom the groom is known, took place at Bolton on Wednesday, Jan. 7th, when Miss Dorothy D. Wakely, until recently vice-principal of Kent School, Toronto. was married to Dr. W. D. Smith (Faculty of Medicine, Toronto, '11), of Creemore. The bride was attended by her cousin, Miss Mary Corbett, of Creemore, while the groom was supported by his brother, Mr. W. M. Smith, of Victoria University. Master George Branton, of Toronto, a cousin of the bride, sang during the signing of the register. Among those present were Miss Kate Campbell, '10, Mr. A. L. Smith, '13. and Mr. D. E. Dean, '11.

Soccer

Victoria Wins the Intermediate Inter-Faculty Soccer Championship

VICTORIA 0—KNOX 0.

On Monday, December 8th, the soccer team again met Knox on the back campus to play off the tie resulting from the previous game. Weather conditions were most unfavorable, ice and snow underfoot and a regular gale blowing down the field. As a result the play was uneven but both goals were well defended, and when full-time was called neither side had scored. Twenty minutes' overtime failed to produce any further result and it was decided to replay the game at an early date. Of the "Vic." men, goalkeeper Brown, and indeed the whole back division, deserve great credit, but Fortune smiled on us once when a shot from one of the Knox forwards caromed off one goal post, hit the other and bounced—out. The line-up was the same as in the following game.

VICTORIA 3—KNOX 2.

On the following Thursday the two teams faced one another in a third attempt to decide the series. The Knox captain changed his line-up in an effort to win the game and his judgment was confirmed when after some minutes of play Cameron scored on a pass from right wing. Shortly after this their right wing again carried the ball down and with a splendid shot Oliver scored a second goal for Knox. At this stage of the game the outlook was far from cheerful for "Vic.," but the forwards repeatedly forced the play down to the Knox end of the field and finally Morley Smith shot cleverly over his head, the surprised goalkeeper made a fatal fumble and " Vic." had scored. At half-time the score stood two to one and in the light of previous games that small lead looked to be enough to win. But in the second half the speed and condition of the Victoria men began to tell and they were rewarded when the Knox goalkeeper in clearing a shot threw the ball fairly at Annsley, who was coming in fast. It rebounded through the posts and the score was tied at two all. Play now became more strenuous, but the "Vic." men were in their stride and on a pass from left wing, Heuther shot, hitting the cross-bar. As the ball bounded back into play one of the Knox men struck it with his arm and a penalty kick was awarded. Annsley was called upon to take the penalty and he responded with a well-timed shot which the Knox goalkeeper had no chance to save. With a margin of one goal and a championship in sight, "Vic." played desperately and for the remaining ten minutes ran their opponents off their feet. Annsley almost scored again, when on receiving a pass he made for the goal via the direct route and missed his shot only by inches. Time was called without change in the score and the championship was ours. The Knox men proved their good sportsmanship, if proof were necessary by being the first to congratulate us. It was a hard game for them to lose but a glorious victory for us.

The celebration which followed may be left to the imagination or memory as the case may be; but a few words of praise are due the captain, manager and members of the team whose faithful work won its merited reward. They will feel doubly rewarded, indeed, if this year's success in any way helps to gain for Soccer the place it merits among the college sports.

The following was the line-up for both games—Goal, Brown; backs, White, M. P. Smith; halves, Marritt, Humphrey, Greer; right wings, Annsley, Heuther; left wings, McCamus, Sanderson; centre, W. M. Smith.

W. R. M.

Water Polo

VICTORIA 5—"SCHOOL" 1.

After losing, unfortunately, by an extremely close margin to Arts the week before, on December 8th, Victoria met School. If we won this game and School defeated Arts the series would be again tied. We fortunately lived up to our part, but School on' the following Friday were unequal to the occasion, and Arts for the second year in succession won the championship and seven valuable silver medals. However, the manner in which we outclassed School in this game and the closeness of the score in the finals show that we are clearly the equals of any team in the league.

"Vic." started with her same team, although several shifts were made, Brewster going to ' the forward line, Duggan to goal and Fleming on the defence. This greatly strengthened the team. A fair crowd was in attendance and gave good support. Brewster scored the most for "Vic." and played a stellar game. Willows was more closely watched by School, than any other of our men, which shows the respect School have for him. Crowe in centre played an admirable game. It is his first season in the game and he has made a distinct success. Centre position is the most tiring place on the team; and, although at times almost exhausted, he gamely continued. Simpson is another man who is playing this year for the first time. He is speedy and an excellent check, and has been very effective on the defence. Manager Duggan gave a grand exhibition in goal, stopping several difficult 'shots. 'School scored the first goal by a long shot within the first thirty seconds of the game, but never afterwards had a "look-in." Crowe, after repeated warnings for "fouling" was given a rest on the side line for half a minute. School pressed hard, but in spite of this handicap we managed to score. The game, all told, was an excellent exhibition and "Vic." deserves great praise for their admirable performance.

Line-up—goal, C. R. Duggan (Mgr.); defence, C. Simpson, R. R. Fleming (Capt.); centre, Crowe; forwards, Willows, H. S. Brewster.

Our College Rink

Now that our second term is well opened and weather prophets are trying to determine whether the January thaw has been or is to be, it would seem that an article on our college rink is not unseasonable. " Little Vic " needs no introduction to the public of Toronto and certainly not to the students of Victoria, and yet it is doubtful if the student body is as closely in touch with the aims and endeavors of the rink management and of the Athletic Executive as is desirable.

The provision for athletics in the college and the management of the campus are delegated by the faculty to the student body. That this trust is a deserved one is shown by the fact that Victoria has at the present time athletic facilities unequalled by any other college in the University. Naturally the expense of upkeep is heavy. In addition to these ordinary expenses the Athletic Executive has a liability in the form of a loan of $8,000, which is the debt outstanding on our new building completed last spring at a total cost of over $13,000. Athletic fees and the rental of lockers are a sure, but rather inadequate source of revenue. The great part of this burden falls upon the rink.

The rink, although it has been under different management every year, has had continued and increasing prosperity. Not only among the student body of the University has it become popular. It has built up a large patronage among all classes of Toronto citizens. Last year, for the first time, the rink had the advantage of really commodious public dressing rooms equipped with all conveniences. In addition to this a new lighting system was installed. This year has seen a new building erected for the accommodation of hockey teams practising at "Little Vic." It is steam heated and equipped with shower baths. Each year's management institutes new improvements for the public convenience, with the result that the athletic organization, through the continued popularity of the rink, is assured of an annual income seldom less than $3,000, and often more.

Every effort is made to compete with other rinks in securing public patronage. Our ice maker, Mr. Whitebread, is, we believe, the best in the city. This year his success was especially marked when " Little Vic " was open for two nights before any of the other open-air rinks. And yet, although we cater to the public, the rink still remains essentially a student rink. It is run by the students for the students and its revenues all go towards increasing the pleasure and athletic opportunities of Victoria students. On this ground the management bases its claim to the hearty support of every man and woman in the college. Let each one look upon the rink with a feeling that they have a share in its success and then " Little Vic " will benefit by that best form of advertising—the enthusiastic support of every student in the college.

Girls' Athletics

The most exciting game of the Intercollegiate Basket-ball Series was that played between St. Hilda's and Victoria on the night of December 8th, in the gymnasium of the Household Science Building. The first score was made by " Vics," when they succeeded in putting in a free shot. Then the St. Hildans made several baskets, but the ball when directed toward the St. Hilda's basket seemed charmed, for repeatedly it rolled round the basket, only to fall off again on the wrong side. At half-time the score was 7—5 in favor of the Anglicans. During the second half St. Hilda's first made a basket, then " Vics," and soon they were tied. The score was next at odds, first one side being ahead, then the other. When there were about two minutes left to play "Vic." was leading, then the score became tied by a successful free shot for the St. Hildans, followed closely by the determining basket which gave them the game. The score was 15—13. This game also gave them the championship for this year, as that was the fourth game they had won, without losing any.

The last game of the series was played with Varsity in the same gym. the night of December 11th. Its issue had no effect upon the championship, consequently it was most friendly. The final score was 12—5 in " Vic's " favor. The line-up for both games was: Forwards, Miss Kenny and Miss Flanders; centres, Miss Thompson, Miss Edwards and Miss Clerk; defence, Miss Luke and Miss Reid.

Great credit is due Mr. W. Zimmerman, of '16, for his tireless work as coach of the team.

The hockey practices have begun, and there will be an inter-year series, as well as the usual inter-collegiate series of games.

Once more we come to the beginning of the end. Now for the grind.

The following are a few New Year resolutions that we have overheard:

That, henceforth, I will deny myself the pleasure of saying my prayers in Hebrew.—E. D. Beynon.

That this year I *will* specialize.—Otto Clipperton.

That I will be the first president of the S.P.C.L. (Society for Prevention of Cruelty in Locals).—Linc. Rice.

That I will not use my pull with the Faculty this year.—Grant Robertson.

That I will continue (as heretofore) " to eliminate petty routine business."—A. E. Roseborough.

That I had better stop training for Varsity First Rugby team and get down to work.—J. W. Taylor.

That I *will* learn the Latin grace.—Tom Greer.

That I will cultivate more animation in conversation.—N. V. Buchanan.

That I will not allow my hair to be cut more than twice a week.—A. McLaughlin.

That I will confine my conversation to Hamilton, football and girls.—Duke Pearson.

That I will make one more frantic effort to stop smoking.—Sandy.

That I will decline to accept the Rhodes Scholarship.—J. P. Magwood.

That I will preach my next sermon on " How to talk and say nothing."—K. V. Stratton.

That I will endow a chair in " tangoing."—J. P. S. Nethercott.

That the subject of my ode for the first week in January shall be " The Whyness of the What."—A. L. Phelps.

That I will endeavor to find a new outlet for my hitherto restricted talents.—A. P. McKenzie.

That I will breathe and think from the diaphragm—Ho! Ho!—Ha! Ha!—Prof. Greaves.

That I will buy a red tie to match my smile.—Prof. De Beaumont.

That I will extend Sunday visiting hours to 11.30 p.m.—Miss Addison.

That I will give no term mark of less than five. It's a point; take it down!—Dr. Snow.

The Christmas examination in Botany proved a source of great distress to some of the Freshmen, but not to Mr. B. L. S—mmers, for while other members of his class were puzzling over the nature of a very small green spot upon a plate of glass, Mr. S., with remarkable sagacity, at once saw what was required, and wrote as his answer: "This is a microscope,—made in Germany."

Class Secretary (at nomination meeting).—Does Mr. Moff—t spell his name f-a-t or f-i-t?

Moff-t, '15·—Well, Mr. President, since a man can't be both "fat" and "fit" please write me down "f-i-t."

The annual Oration contest, which was held on Monday evening, December 8th, brought out a number of excellent speakers, but a very small audience. The contest was won by Mr. Collins, of '17, who delivered in excellent style a very interesting address on the topic: "What is Socialism?" Mr. H. L. Sanders, '17, was awarded second place.

The committee in charge of the contest has made a recommendation to the Literary Society that this contest be discontinued owing to the lack of interest. We can hardly think that such a step would be advisable, as the Oration contest is undoubtedly of great benefit to those who participate in it, but it is certain that if the contest is to be continued some innovation must be made in order to attract the interest of a larger portion of the student body.

Flem—ng, '15 (becoming eloquent in Oration contest).—
"Character alone, I say, cannot be assailed by anything in
this universe,—or in any other universe."

Locals offers a grand prize of ten cents for the best trans-
lation of the following motto: "Pas d'elle yeux Rhône que nous."
Professors and students of the Honor Moderns Department
are debarred from this contest.

On Wednesday afternoon, December 17th, we were honored by a visit from Sir Wilfrid Laurier, who addressed a
large gathering of the students in the Dining Hall. It is the
intention of the Faculty to secure a number of prominent
men to address the students of the College in the new hall
from time to time; but we are all proud that the first speaker
to address us from this platform was a man who has served
his country so well, and is held in so high esteem by all Canadians, whatever their political faith may be.

Now that skating is once again occupying the chief attention of the student body, we would humbly suggest to the
Faculty that they should install a clock in the main hall so
that the students may lose no time in getting out to the rink.

The Lit. elections which were held on Saturday, December
13th, resulted in the unprecedented condition of a split ticket,
three Democratic and three Independent candidates being
elected. The officers elected were:—Hon. Pres., Dr. Locke;
Pres., C. W. Smythe; Vice-Pres., S. M. Beach; Critic, A. P.
McKenzie; Leader of Government, R. S. Rodd; Treasurer,
H. Bennett; Secretary, J. P. Nethercott. As the Democrats
secured two of the three cabinet offices, they will occupy the
Government benches during the spring term. A very great
interest was shown in this election and a remarkable amount
of political genius, hitherto unsuspected, was uncovered. We
are reminded in this connection of the words of Sir Wilfrid
Laurier, at the recent Arts banquet, when he said that: Of
methods for bringing voters to the polls he had some knowledge, but of methods for keeping other voters away he knew

nothing, although he had heard of it. We wonder if all the "Vic." campaigners could say as much?

On the back of the note book of a returned delegate to Kansas City we found the outline of some worthy gentleman's speech, which culminated in the equation: Christianity= Sunlight. A local wag, whose name we refuse to divulge, had deduced the analogy somewhat further, and had added: Mohammedanism=Sapolio; Buddhism=Old Dutch Cleanser.

W. N. H-nna, '17 (at South Hall, 10.30 p.m.)—Come on now, be a sport. I'll toss a copper with you, whether you let the girls go down-town for ice-cream.

Mrs. Sheffield (wiltingly).—"Young man, I never gamble."

At Ryrie's store, just before Christmas—"Excuse me, but can you tell me in what department I can find Mr. Bish—p, a student from Victoria College?

Floorwalker—"Certainly, sir. Over there in the whisky flasks!"

Oh, John, we wouldn't have believed it of you!

A TRAGEDY. ACT I. SC. I.

Place—In front of Middle House, Burwash Hall.
Time—Any old time at all.
Dramatis Persona—Lester P—rson's small brother.

(Enter D. P. (dramatis persona.)

"Hello Neil! Hello Gord! Hello Art! Hello Linc! Hello Harry! (Repeated several times in loud voice.)

Mr. M—ssey—"What the ....!"
D. P. (cheerfully)—"Hello Vincent!"
Exit D. P. à la double. Curtain.

Victoria's debating prowess has been shown to be of no inferior calibre by the results achieved by her debating teams during the Michaelmas term. In the Inter-Faculty series Victoria was first pitted against Knox College. On Nov. 13th, Messrs. A. E. McCutcheon, B.A., and C. W. Smythe, '14 upholding the affirmative, triumphed over the Knox representatives, the subject being: "Resolved that the Canadian Government would be justified in entirely prohibiting the immigration of natives from the British Possessions in India." In the semi-finals on Dec. 15th, St. Michael's College opposed Victoria: Messrs. E. E. Pugsley, C.T., and L. G. Hutton, '15., of Victoria, successfully maintained the affirmative of the subject: "Resolved, that the members of the Canadian Senate should be elected for a limited term, and not, as at present, appointed by the Crown."

Meantime, in the Inter-University series, Toronto University was represented in the struggle against Queen's by two of our Victoria men, Messrs. A. L. Smith, B.A. and W. M. Smith, '14. On Nov. 27th, they journeyed to Kingston and managed to beat the Presbyterians. The Varsity representatives upheld the negative of the subject: "Resolved that at the present stage of Canada's development, the missionary efforts of her churches should be confined wholly to the Home Field." Toronto University thus enters the finals against Ottawa University for the Inter-University Debating championship.

Victoria's remaining task is to win the final debate against Trinity College for the possession of the Inter-Faculty championship, and the coveted Kerr Shield. Messrs. W. F. Bowles, '14, and H. A. Hall, '15, two excellent men, have been chosen for the combat and will be given the enthusiastic support of the whole college.

Mention "Acta." Advertisers appreciate it

OFFICIAL CALENDAR OF THE DEPARTMENT
OF EDUCATION FOR THE YEAR 1913.
DECEMBER

1. Last day for appointment of School Auditors by Public and Separate School Trustees. (On or before 1st December).
   Township Clerk to furnish to the School Inspector information of average assessment, etc., of each School Section. (On or before 1st December).
   Legislative grant payable to Trustees of Rural Public and Separate Schools in Districts, second instalment. (On or before 1st December).
8. Model School Final Examination begins.
9. Returning officers named by resolution of Public School Board. (Before 2nd Wednesday in December).
   Last day for Public and Separate School Trustees to fix places for nomination of Trustees. (Before 2nd Wednesday in December).
12. Model Schools close. [Model School Syllabus.]
13. Local assessment to be paid Separate School Trustees. (Not later than 14th Dec.).
15. County Council to pay $500 to High School and Continuation School where Agricultural Department is established. (On or before 15th December).
   Municipal Councils to pay Municipal Grants to High School Boards. (On or before 15th December).
19. Normal Schools (first term) close. [Normal School syllabus].
22. High Continuation, Public and Separate Schools close. (End 22nd December).
25. Christmas Day (Thursday).
   New Schools, alterations of School boundaries and consolidated Schools go into operation or take effect. (Not to take effect before 25th December).
31. Annual meetings of supporters of Public and Separate Schools. (Last Wednesday in December).
   High School Treasurers to receive all moneys collected for permanent improvements. (On or before 31st December).
   Protestant Separate School Trustees to transmit to County Inspectors names and attendance during the last preceding six months. (On or before 31st December).
   Auditors' Report of cities, towns and incorporated villages to be published by Trustees. (At end of year).
   Financial statement, report of attendance, etc., from Teachers' Institutes. (Not later than 31st December).
   Report on Inspectoral visits from Separate, County, and District Inspectors, due. (Not later than December 31st).

Mention "Acta." Advertisers appreciate it.

STOLLERY'S CORRECT EVENING DRESS CHART

OCCASION	COAT AND OVERCOAT	WAISTCOAT	TROUSERS	HAT
EVENING WEDDING BALL RECEPTION FORMAL DINNER AND THEATRE	Swallowtail Cape Paletot or Chesterfield Overcoat	White Single Breasted of Piqué Linen or Silk	Same Material as Coat	High Silk with Broad Felt Band
	COLLAR	CRAVAT	GLOVES	BOOTS
	Poke or Small Square-Tabbed Wing	Small Tab Wing Poke or Lapfront	White Glacé with Self Backs or White Chevreau. White Chamois for Theatre	Patent Leather Buttoned Cloth or Kid Tops Patent Leather Pumps

Compiled by STOLLERY, Yonge and Bloor Streets

The Feel is in the Air for Overcoats

T HE early cool spells are really more trying on the constitution than later on when you expect the cold weather as a regular thing.

NOW IS THE TIME TO BUY AN OVERCOAT

Whether it be a medium weight or a good solid one for winter use, our immense range of patterns and fabrics makes it easy for you to select a coat, and our range of prices has been graded so that every man can buy one. even if his price be as low as $7.50. College Boys will be pleased with our Nifty Models and we will allow you ten per cent. off all purchases if you just mention this advertisement.

OAK HALL CLOTHIERS
Canada's Best All-Clothing Store
COR. YONGE & ADELAIDE STS.,   **J. C. COOMBES, Mgr.**

Mention "Acta." Advertisers appreciate it.

Lightning Source UK Ltd.
Milton Keynes UK
UKHW011144051118
331792UK00005B/422/P